SARAH C

An Arbitrary Line

Broken Sleep Books
brokensleepbooks.com

Published 2018,
Broken Sleep Books:
Talgarreg, Ceredigion, Wales

brokensleepbooks.com

First Edition

Lay out your unrest.

Publisher/Editor: Aaron Kent
Editor: Charlie Baylis

Typeset in UK by Aaron Kent

Broken Sleep Books is committed to
a sustainable future for our planet,
and therefore uses print on
demand publication.

brokensleepbooks@gmail.com

ISBN: 9781790245499

An Arbitrary Line is restlessly inventive with formal possibility and visually complex in its desire to extend itself through narrative and philosophical meditation. A reader will find many ways into the poem's rich and textured surface where concrete and typographical escapades disrupt and extend the lyric imaginings of this adventure into the ice and snow of the archive. The poem hangs like a necklace strung around its various found gems and flickering shards copied from Lady Franklin's nineteenth-century journal that pattern this new collection from Sarah Cave.
– Redell Olsen

Both Cave and Slava are shamans, journeying into language, delusion, spirit worlds, and lands of impulse, faith and doubt.
– Rupert Loydell

An Arbitrary Line takes us into a rare spiritual struggle, at once circumspect and innocent, in dialogue with its own contradiction like all properly tested faith; the 'reasonable sacrifice' of the hermetic life which never sacrifices reason itself. Within the images and swerves of its deceptively concise phrasing, its seeming anachronisms and Absurdist flourishes we find a consciousness which is timeless, prayerful and fully human. Also it's funny. Do you have any idea how difficult it is making material like this funny without losing its soul, its focus and ultimate deep seriousness? It's really difficult. A jaw-dropping first collection from a talent I hope to be reading for many years.
– Luke Kennard

AN ARBITRARY LINE

Slava is a religious hermit living on an archipelago in the Russian Arctic where the coastline is shaped by millions of years of heavy weather, erosion and geological disruption. Slava has lost radio contact with his monastery and everything that was, is and will be is now only memory. Slava's world starts to disintegrate and madness and hunger blur the lines between sand and ice. Fragments of memory and experience merge and there is little distinction between body and landscape, human and non-human, Slava and non-Slava.

'… a condemned man, just before he died, said, or thought, that if he had to live on some high crag, on a ledge so small that there was no more room for his two feet, with all about him the abyss, the ocean, eternal night, eternal solitude, eternal storm, and there he must remain, on a hand's breadth of ground, all his life, a thousand years, through all eternity – it would be better to live so, than die within the hour.'

— *Crime and Punishment*, Dostoyevsky

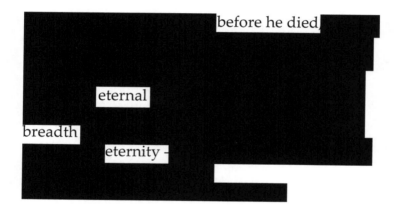

before he died,

eternal

breadth

eternity –

Dawn
emerges

light
bleeds

blue
mist

Last contact ● was beginning voices

known /unknown ● tracing statistics

long wire ● distance no — where there
birds are unwritten   analogue
dabs of silt ● mapping bird flight

Watching the Clock #1
5 a.m. (transcribed from Lady Franklin's Archive at the Scott Polar Institute, Cambridge)

'Morning star we commend
our king to thee. Be to him
a sun and shield. The clock
has now struck five.
Come then mild sun
from the distant pole
and shine on us and our home.'

Giant **flightless bird**
six feet tall

studies polar activity
his observations made
in Morse code
his beak clicking

he holds matchstick ships

in place

while machine tells him
where mussels can be found

bottles drift the surf
and flightless bird
uses his huge beak

to munch
through leaves,
nuts, seeds and fruit

1.
Sun as Shield

Slava, the monk, crumbles in atmosphere. He is pre-reformation, reforming orogeny. He turns seven roses to dust, particles renovate space junk leaving signs in the sky read by re-novitiate oracles. Dissolution of brimstone; a sun-black dreamscape of dissolving snake.

1
A bear encounters
Slava, a fox
in dark outline

2
Slava unfolds
in shadows

cast on ice

3
Slava's bittern
beak finds
grubs and slugs

4
Daily compline
is an exchange

many molluscs
pass between
Slava and bittern

Encounter   Be(ar)

on the shore   on   moving   on the shore she came

white   like the sky   white   like the ground   white

like the horizon

and so they named one another

and the bear didn't turn
the light didn't turn
his obscured still life form
blackening her coat
and stifling the oil lamp

and then turn

to the   left

she to the   right

our   noses
  rubbedtogether

Diseases of the brain

conceal her absence
from the tunnelled hearth
the adobe walls reveal her
earthenware paw-language
the cubs are now bones
picked clean by her

mouthing combined flesh
their parallel disintegration
a sexual intercourse resembling
being animal
             -Slava
from Slava
             -animal   ~~(did we turn the lights off?)~~

A Misreading

reading Lady Franklin's handwriting in the Scott Polar Institute

Painted red in general except the ground on which
disguise in high relief causes a painted black upon
white grounds or white upon black. I would give
so much to be able to draw chickens in cages.

Encountering the bear
at the window
lifts Slava from meditation
the glass from its frame

reflections **shatter-**

                    red in communion

Slava's **ruined face**

Island Notes
FOSSILS SHOW PARENTAL CARE

> As it broke them apart
the world was mostly ice free.
> DNA read in migration
patterns during day.
> Far away hard to reach
Slava remembers his father.
> Far away hard to reach
Slava remembers his father.
> Far away hard to reach
~~Slava remembers his father.~~
> Meeting beneath the aurora
they match their bones.

Matchstick World's

hum, hm?

     the generator's
hum soothes cowled ears.

Slava fiddles with matchsticks
recreating Hyperborea/Cornucopia

the stilted viewing platforms
the sock-muffled gramophone

filling the hut
with oscillations
of Pechoran sea and divine prophesy
the world – a sauna
               birch wood strikes
`against flesh`
            bathing in warmth
dry currents   desert parents crunch

flightless birds in their steaming swamps

eternal light // pinprick night

cages but no chickens just cages
a warning in flight
Slava sleeps exposed on the dunes

it's raining toads
and yoghurt pots   (.)

Skin clad curragh
shifts between islands
polyarnik #amwriting
from the heronry

seeking meaning
seeking names
seeking conversation
            with rocks

that reveal

the depth   of Him

of our

not to be   his own

'lost growing
sense of amnesia'

#**polyarniknotes**

swigging liquor
from a carton

claiming incidents
in lost form

Granite shelves
yellow-faced

the heron
his habit
wings protect

the lighthouse
with its vision
seeks him

solitary
among the reeds

Watching the Clock #2

4 a.m. (transcribed from Lady Franklin's Archive at the Scott Polar Institute, Cambridge)

'To thou, o God, be our honour.
Thou art our guardian
while we remain on earth.
The watchmen now depart
for his protection during night.
Return our thanks to God
and profit by the new day.'

floating negotiates
primitive

plantation

hunched in cowl
counts
rockpool bottles
a quartz glimmer
blue marble
withered glass
oat shell
strings of clinging

spools

the sour smell
of Slava

in decay

Message in a Bottle #1

Caterpillars bask in sunlight
curling their toes...

Do caterpillars have toes?

2.
Magic Lantern
(memento mori)

Slava holds magic lantern images
up to the hurricane lamp

Scheherazade's stillness
chipped wallpaper
black silhouettes
Konstantin
Slava

Konstantin
Slava

Konstantin
Slava

slides switching
with speed

Slava wakes the rain
blurred circular window
a nightlife of wailing seal
a turmoil of mating grief

Slava sees fierceness
in his visions

memories of renovation
and rejection

all the while the scene turns

                his gaze
settling on a drowned vixen

a curtain of rain closes in

     moonlight
behind black vapour

The Lighthouse

Fluorescence skims water,
                              the shoreline
puckers with ice.
            Konstantin, a thick band of wool
            pulled tight to his skin, watches
            obscure
                silhouettes on the horizon. He
            strains
            his mind, seeking
middle ground, middle meaning, middle –
            middle.

Night-time pilgrim
a solitary wrecker
lamp drooping
a donkey's tail
along rough inlets
low lying sea ice
Seven Seals
wait in the cove
their dark eyes
absorbing Slava

Coastal Vinyl

Fossils find themselves in rhythms
deposited in records

their medium   **is** free-voice jazz
experiment
no Strauss   distressed
Johann   cliff face
Richard   wailing

remixed Pinnipeds

not always an appreciative
audience

                  suggesting fossil-jazz
is an acquired taste   a rich tea sediment

c. 1970s   kitsch referendum

'Don't play what's there; play what's not there.'
                              — Miles Davis

The bear returns
litter…   Slava

an egg

cannot recall regurgitation

He remembers the ticks

but now   //   no response

he cracks   //   hatched

a gull's egg

eating the content

contemplating

the jagged remains

cutting his finger

On shell

Watching the Clock #3
3 a.m. (transcribed from Lady Franklin's Archive at the Scott Polar Institute, Cambridge)

'Now the night will soon
be past and the day begun.
Let all be banished
who wish to make us sorry.
The clock has now struck three.
O great father assist us
and grant to us thy love.'

Saint Anthony of Siya's

                    grey-green
haggard eyes
avail in leaves

paternal refuge
ragged wanderer

forged to die (.) alone

he brings in the harvest

the fearful monk
scything corn

men of family and hearth
once saw Anthony's light
as distant sub-species

The Fox Confessor

The fox pulls the curtain shut.

Priest: What is it my son?

The fox shivers, ragged candlelight falls through the grate singeing his coat, burnt yellow; dark pupils where something else dances into form.

Fox: I have nothing.

Slava watches
from the boat
petroleum
light refracts
  slick shine
patch of water.
He guides the boat
gently towards it.
He dips his carton
into the murk

drinks greedily

The cloud
is little known
keep covered
in ocean spray

by
a
black
rain
cloud
hymnal

Naming the stone
after Robert Lax

stone

is clear

ing of

mind

slow

deep

voice

makes

horizon

dim-

lit

orison

bear

able

3.
Day Begins
(~~before~~/after/~~during~~ compline)

The monastery stands in ruins. A soviet guard pauses beneath a green and yellow light display. Six hundred miles north east, the young monk and former libertine, Konstantin, is an apparition in the dark mirror of Slava.

Watching the Clock #4

2 a.m. (transcribed from Lady Franklin's Archive at the Scott Polar Institute, Cambridge)

'Benevolent Jesus
who loves us so much,
in this dark wilderness,
teach us to know thy worth.
To you belongs all honour.'

Konstantin orders coffee
dark and thick

and snow falls
on **Nevsky Prospect**

Anton Chekhov, in a dust coat,
fresh from scene painting,
arrives – eats cake – tells

Konstantin that the world
is almost finished

Konstantin looks worried
and repeats

'the world is almost finished'

Meanwhile,

Grandmother Proletkult

            lies quiet
in the soiled snow

Nevsky
            Prospect

divides her children

born
to
rags

now in furs

sold to the ballet
or the church
to avoid the fatal

mix of vodka
tramline and cold

the lines where Proletkult's
warmth is cooled
to the callous

'The Christian who is a socialist is to be dreaded
far more than the socialist who is an atheist.'

– Dostoyevsky

```
    –  Slava  remembers  books
       Types  fragments
       among  the  silver  reeds
```

```
Binary  code
```

black/white/black/white/black/white

there are no line breaks in Slava's life / only breath

'This lake could be
anywhere'   repeats Slava

changing tenses
these waters were once populated
by
          isolated man

a heron   thumping

a driftwood ballad

speaking in long lines
of
mysticism

a rockpool elegy   **a one stone reprieve**

leaving behind the tousled Nina

and the flustered Sunday afternoons
before attendance was compulsory

the conclusion
to faith holding hands with doubt

Slava watches the evening   and waits

for the yearly melt

as inevitable

as the changing of the skyline

                    reflected
                        in lakes, of lakes,
                vast open absence

by the lake/ in the lake/ of the lake

glacial foundations mocked

Konstantin fights his corner
up to his shirt sleeves

in the rising   / lake
Nina plays the riverbank chords

a xylophone minuet of lakes
lakes lakes near lakes eventual lakes

many lakes melting

water/ ocean turning

stomach churned
and in the freeze frame of future history

monks paddle through milk-sea
and plastic waste

Fatherhood in Three Connective Panels

            1
Konstantin's cradle
flightless wings loom above
Scheherezade's

matchstick crow feasting
on eggshell

            2
Anton's black feathers
askew   a dull murmur
of morning

Konstantin brings light
feeds Anton soft entrails
still warm   the rabbit

now cold

            3
Absent fathers

        Konstantin
becomes Slava
his life is dancing
leaves fallacious
prophesy

An arbitrary line
drawn in Slava's
mind definition
of island-man
and mainland
is made unreal
by storm

erosion, rocks
salt, shell, quartz

Face
less
fig
ures   loom/dusty
              tund
              ra
              dry
              ice/fragmented
              history

Cep
ha
lap
sis   would
                 have
                 grinned
                 at
                 the
                 joke

but he was jaw
              less

Downward Melody
          Or, *the science of hot air balloons and ice*

They had to create their own world
visible from the air

woolly mammoth drawn carriages
translucent people

words harnessed by thick furred
mammals stripped

a sideways glimmer of rotting gum
and false optimism

crazed toasting of champagne saved
from the wreck

wicker and sail

a flimsy offering to an ocean that longs
to be sky

Slava sleeps peacefully as men perish

'It is not a question of two hundred or three hundred years, for even after a million years life will still be exactly the same as it was before. Life does not change, it remains constant, following its own particular laws, laws which are outside your scope or, at the very least, laws which you will never know. Migratory birds, cranes for example, keep on flying and flying, and no matter what thoughts wander into their heads, whether they are sublime or petty it is no matter, they will still keep on flying and not know why they are flying or where they are flying to. They fly and will keep on flying whatever philosophers might be born amongst them; and let them philosophise, as much as they wish, as long as they keep on flying.'

– *The Three Sisters*, Anton Chekhov

Destination. Moscow?

Sorry, we could not calculate directions from
"Khodovarikha, Nenets Autonomous Okrug, Russia,
166715" to "Moscow, Russia"
#Googlemaps

Message in a Bottle #2

A letter to the Tsar,

How do you address a Tsar?

Negotiating Raptor

The Eagle: You in me. I in you.

The romance could not last for long. Strong talons gripped Slava's cheek bones. Half decapitation, half embrace.

Slava: Save me.

Bewick's Swan

Lines in wood
the block is carved
the word is written
the swan watches
back the last migration
in fascination before
pressure is seizure

of white space

Watching the Clock #5

1 a.m. (transcribed from Lady Franklin's Archive at the Scott Polar Institute, Cambridge)

'Jesus, instruct us all
to hear our woe tonight;
thou art the only saviour.
The clock now struck one,
uphold thy arm over us
and we shall conquer all.'

(68.475925, 28.47013)
Finland

Rajoosepintie, Inari, Finland.
Verkhnetulomskaya doroga,   Tree birch and
sky. Tarmac rolls.   Murmanskaya,
Russia.   Raja-Joosepi.
Borderland. Before   **Access**
Denied.   the barrier,
homeland, surface
rhythms penetrated by familiarity.
Boundaries forever regressing. Man
wearing warm once-mink hat stops traffic.

188734 Leningrad Oblast, Russia:
54920 Taipalsaari, Finland

Further south   Saimaa Seals are beyond borders

Ladoga
    Saimaa

    Ladoga
    Saimaa typewriter memory

    Ladoga
    Saimaa

                oil slick heads make a bid
for pre-Ice age freedom via man-made canal

4.
Remains of Midsummer

The Monks move westward, sun slants through blades of open canopy, ecstatic visions of life stand an arm's stretch above. The forest clears for lakes and churches but slowly reclaims them, like a father giving away his daughter. Slava laughs as Nina fades to dancing bloom.

Yearly pilgrimage   Slava-birds rise
caught out

monks walk   across the flooded
sackcloth landscape

waterscape

risen drunk on high summer
fruits grown in solitude
picking

Konstantin appears   at the church
with fern fronds –
the need-fire barring the entrance –

Slava fades   **to archipelago**

Pale purple lavender
nesting tundra
sun and moon meet
dark box

light slits   tinfoil midsummer

sage purges

     Slava   the heron
     emerges from the fumes

Wilderness   Church

(68.951464, 27.115524)

Pielpajärven   **erämaakirkko**

Slava remembers the uncurling of the leaf. Holy
starches grow sunwards. He wiggles his caterpillar
crochet hooks before becoming chrysalis.

Slava stands
a solitary spruce

after the leaves
before the snow

Trees state
ecologists, seen
illegally wearing
(cassocks)
will bring the bear
Seraphim fed
to factory natural
Eastern value
small details of forest/
Nicean Creed
          distant
parliament commands
land approval earth yoke
to spill across Slava's
worn haircloth

      birch-scape

Slava lurks in
seed cone
teaching the telling

What will caterpillars
do **but dive for sponges?**

The monk plucks
feathers from

a long-tailed
duck standing

between swamp
and mountain

Lenin crosses
the border

a **Finnish
melancholy**

lies limply
eyeless

doubt now
borderless

A dried
treasury   a solitary
stem rescued
        from the flames

from the summer
        the **Wilderness**
Church
        stills the memory
        stills the sweetness
of cloud berries
and burning myrtle

Watching the Clock #6
12 a.m. (transcribed from Lady Franklin's Archive at the Scott
Polar Institute, Cambridge)

'It was at midnight that
Jesus Christ was born.
Never forget that hour;
without his coming
the world would not be saved.
The clock has now struck twelve;
we commend ourselves to God.'

Avalonia

Spiral bookcase   forming staircase
              the tower's ascent

                    red lines are sutures
                    mist damp cool
                    water on Slava's skin

a finger caresses the dust
capitalised names
pages decay

                    Slava strikes a match
                              holds it to the shroud.

'Do not weep:
Heaven fashioned us of nothing, and we strive
to bring ourselves to nothing.'
                    – The Duchess of Malfi, John Webster

Fear
for Moominpappa

A mechanism sparse
prayer   absence   loss
the periphery of the orb
kept   –   the keeper
          lights the way
          the drowning
     the near-drowned
those who know nothing
of apophatic depths
feel only surface
revolution before
morning dims the lamp

and what is not
returns

Beneath a ridge of granite
Slava fashioned a **limpet crucifix**
and sucked his fingers clean
tasting sea life fade to death

Wearing only **the mask
of a heron** Slava sits
on a rock, arms
raised to the sky, echoing
a thousand nights of painful
ecstasy for the feeding
of the bear

Scattered outline
of heron now dancing
monk in the granular
filter of Lark's Midsummer

eremitic man's
dissent   against sky-CLOUD

5.
A Happy End

Konstantin wears his Slava-suit in the noonday
heat, pulls at the rope-tie hope about his neck, asks
for salt water and prays for the weightless
nightingale who signals the falling light; the
candle snuffed before bed time.

Watching the Clock #7
11 p.m. (transcribed from Lady Franklin's Archive at the Scott
Polar Institute, Cambridge)

'God our father watch us all
whether we are great
or small enclose
us with thy arms
protect the city, our house
and home. May we never
forget God during our hours
on earth.'

Tango Magnolia

The Bear: The news of your misbehaviour makes me suffer enormously.

The Bear *moves toward* Slava *hypnotically, an undercurrent of notes in minor, his kalimavkion slides from side to side.* Slava's *eyes twitch, sewn shut, his head cast down, supplicant to the Word. In hold, he and bear, a mauling rhythm with a series of aggressive turns.*

Slava: I will try to relieve your sufferings.

What makes sin?

Sin **is** despair
Slava weeps

Sin is intensified weakness
Slava sighs

Sin is intensified defiance
Slava rages

Slava is sin
Slava dances in candlelight

Konstantin and Nina
court like cranes

in circles

one curling

the other

in reeds   among the dunes

the heron

whispers future past perfect
and Nina tears out br
ee
aa
ss
tt feathers

Konstantin will become

Slava   and join the monastery
and find true love   for a
time

Slava-existence is sin

Slava-existence is sin

Slava-existence is sin

Slava-existence is sin

Slava-existence is sin

Slava-existence is sin

Slava-existence is sin

Slava **will be** sin.

6.
Mermaid Curve

There have been visitations by women, half-clothed in human form, in the bay at Lovns Bredning. Konstantin visits Ørslev Kloster, a Benedictine nunnery near Aalborg, where he compromises his relationship with Nina. Den Lille Havfrue sings without words for her lost lover and shatters her shell collarbone on the rocks.

Mermaid as fabulous animal
Mermaid as man-made skeleton
Mermaid as pieced together
         all different parts

Still   she   waits

the outline of streets

the outline of streets
in Copenhagen contort

u
 n
  n
   a
    t
     u
  y l l a r

u
 n
  n
   a
    t
     u
  y l l a r

and stretch

the outline of streets
over indifferent

u
 n
  n
   a
    t

landscapes
following   enlightened rows

lines of reason   no path   the city adopts
architecture   snow-covered

u
 l   r
   a

birches

double exposure   restrained by another

Konstantin tries to look beyond the harbour,
beyond the mermaid curve of land, beyond
industrial buildings, yachts and pleasure cruisers,
beyond the coast guard to where fields of white
crosses stand knee-deep in water, their turbines
whirr   with   reverie

'Not everyone likes big cities' says den Lille Havfrue.

Slava, waist deep in the gulf, washes his face in silt.

Watching the Clock #8
10 p.m. (transcribed from Lady Franklin's Archive at the Scott Polar Institute, Cambridge)

'If you will know the hour,
martyr, maid, and boy,
the time is coming
that you must go to bed
and deliver up to God.
Be fair and good, take
care of candle and of fire,
our clock has struck ten.'

Hagiography of Ice

Sea
son
cold
white,
white
grey
blue
fade
to eye

white
wit
ness
no
thing

No   cinemas
no   theatres
no   galleries
no   taxis

in **bird land**   this land

Slava-land   Slava loosened

a lost soul

threads of cow bearing

wild laughter
        split mirror

Glass has returned to sand, time slips to the floor. Slava is thinking only of sand. Grains stream through his fingers, empty eyelet windows. Workers once slept here – **living by the light** – before the monks came.

7.
Dark Wilder-n-e-S-s

A deathbed silence – your teeth by the bed, a posthumous smile – is sand.

Watching the Clock #9
9 p.m. (transcribed from Lady Franklin's Archive at the Scott Polar Institute, Cambridge)

'Now that day is past
and night begins,
forgive us all our sins.
For thy son Jesus' sake
protect our house
and all those in our land
from our evening's invasion.'

desert. Coastline

mist   horizon concealed   mist

against face   solitude   silence

                        solitude   silence
the tower   mist   the tower   mist
a bird alights   long legs   a bird alights

vertical. Coastline

mist   mist   mist   mist
mist   mist   mist   mist
mist   mist   mist   mist
horizon   hidden   in
mist   mist   mist   mist
mist   mist   mist   mist
plain   sight   against
solitude   silence
silence   solitude
mist   mist   mist   mist
though   which   the
mist   mist   mist   mist
mist   mist   mist   mist
mist   mist   mist   mist
frames   the   alighting
mist   mist   mist   mist
long   legs   of   a   bird
alighting   through
mist   mist   mist   mist
to   the   tower

Reversed Catechism

In this dark wilderness, do we walk?
an abandoned home

This is what makes the world dark.

In this dark wilderness, do we seek?
concealed in rock pools

This is what makes the world dark.

In this dark wilderness, are we tender?
shells broken at night

This is what makes the world dark.

In this dark wilderness, are we obscured?
moon making milk of darkness

This is what makes the world dark.

Slava remembers **the last supply ship** bringing cigarettes, Scotch, letters from friends and wipes clear mucus cresting his blue eyes. A ragged printer's roll leaves its last impression on the horizon.

clouds   clouds

un   thinking
knowing

un   knowing
thinking

risen   Slava
disused
light   is only
housing   candle

         prayer seen

through misted

Claude glass

the cabin
the cave
the sauna

these shores are the last resting place

of the tabernacle
and our search -
pre-monarch
for the **razor clam**

H
i
s

h
e
a
d

a

t
e
n
d
e
r

unfolding

Watching the Clock #10
8 p.m. (transcribed from Lady Franklin's Archive at the Scott Polar Institute, Cambridge)

'When the dark begins
and the day disappears
it reminds us of our latter hour.
Depart us Jesus until death
and give us all a happy end.'

Slava couldn't remember how **the curtain** had come to divide the room

no coffin, many crows
an **afterword** to

Slava

The Goose

'Does all time end here?' asks the goose, eyes closed, pink tears. 'Does it gather in the natural curl of this sanddune, the curve of your thigh, drumming seven oil can harmonies for its last moments?' Slava slits its middle and purple innards stain the decking.

'I don't think about death. When my time comes
I won't care. Life's fine as it is, why think about
death? Why spoil the time you're given?'

– Vyacheslav Korotki,
Khodovarikha, Russia

Acknowledgements

Gratitude to the editors of *The Clearing, Stride, Tears in the Fence, Shearsman,* and *X-Peri* for publishing poems from this collection. A warm thank you to Rupert Loydell, Isabel Galleymore, Jen Hadfield, Luke Kennard, Redell Olsen, Nathan Thompson, Luke Thompson, Alex Badman-King, Annabel Banks, and Anna Cathenka for supporting the book at various stages of its development. Thank you to Aaron Kent and Broken Sleep for having the faith.

I owe a creative debt to the Scott Polar Archive, Robert Lax, and the artwork of Evgenia Arbugaeva, whose photographs of the Polyarnik Vyacheslav Korotkin inspired the character of Slava.

Lastly, thank you Slava

LAY OUT YOUR UNREST

15277082R00053

Printed in Great Britain
by Amazon